How God Ends Us

DéLana R. A. Dameron

Foreword by Elizabeth Alexander

THE UNIVERSITY OF SOUTH CAROLINA PRESS

Published in Cooperation with the South Carolina Poetry Initiative, University of South Carolina

Published by the University of South Carolina Press
Columbia, South Carolina 29208

www.sc.edu/uscpress

Manufactured in the United States of America

18 17 16 15 14 13 12 11 10 09   10 9 8 7 6 5 4 3 2 1

Library of Congress Cataloging-in-Publication Data

Dameron, DéLana R. A.
    How God ends us / DéLana R. A. Dameron ; foreword by Elizabeth
Alexander.
        p. cm. — (Winners of the South Carolina poetry book prize)
    "Published in cooperation with the South Carolina Poetry Initiative,
University of South Carolina."
    ISBN 978-1-57003-832-7 (pbk. : alk. paper)
    I. Title.
    PS3604.A4398H68 2009
    811'.6—dc22

                                                            2008053396

This·book was printed on Glatfelter Natures, a recycled paper with 30 percent
postconsumer waste content.

The South Carolina Poetry Book Prize is given annually to the manuscript that
wins the contest organized and sponsored by the South Carolina Poetry Initiative.
The winning title is published by the University of South Carolina Press in coop-
eration with the South Carolina Poetry Initiative.

The quotation on p. 3, opening part 1, is from Stephen Adly Guirgis, *Jesus Hopped
the "A" Train*. The quotation on p. 27, opening part 2, is from Cesar Vallejo, *Los
Heraldos Negros* (The Black Messengers). The quotation on p. 59, opening part 3,
is from Erica Hunt, "Corolary Artist (1)."

For Daddy, Mama, and Sissy (Thomas W. Dameron Jr.,
Lavoris Renà Dameron, and Tressa T. L. Dameron)

For my grandmother Louise B. Melvin and my aunt
Jenniese Carr and the rest of the living Beltons
and Melvins and Damerons

See the Lord is going to lay waste
the earth and devastate it;
he will ruin its face
and scatter its inhabitants

Isaiah 24:1

The world turns,
who made the sun,
who owns the sea?
the world we know
will fall piece by piece.
all illusions shattered.

Tracy Chapman,
"Paper and Ink"

Contents

III

Foreword

DéLana Dameron's fine book *How God Ends Us* makes unfamiliar poetic music. I chose this manuscript as the first-prize winner of the South Carolina Poetry Book Prize from among many fine gatherings of poems. What distinguished it at first was the rich mystery of the speaking voice. Dameron listens to her own strange music and plays it. That is what her craft serves, and that is what her artistic courage enables:

> Inside the tender part—the stomach of a lie—
> are other kept silences. How You twirl
> Your fiery tongue. Your words are smoke.
> But, how You'll end us,
> summon spirits from inhabitable spaces
> to whisper the beginnings of disaster.
>
> (from "Lament")

For it is courageous indeed to be able to present the personae that Dameron does: speakers who are concerned with listening and seeing, observing, and self-scrutinizing. Her speakers are ruthless with the poem-making self but filled with compassion for the world they encounter. "Inheritance," a poem worth quoting in full, reveals this quality:

> Frequented in dreams
> by fresh-dead loves, so I have seen
> with these eyes the eyes of a spirit

who's crossed, seen the body reject
its coffin bed and climb right out
onto the church's plank floor
seen the dove at the bed's foot
calling out all names, or the red eyes
of the flesh, abandoned. Do not say
I should be grateful for perfect eyes
or their ability to see such distances.
Say I should be grateful for sight,
for open and shut.

That compassion, however, is never sentimental. Rather it is true compassion, in the poet's steady and unwavering gaze.

The syntax of these poems is wonderfully peculiar and exact. The poems raise questions they cannot always answer, real questions the poems themselves explore. Stylistically Dameron understands the function and power of the elliptical, which she uses to great effect in this book.

These poems are beautiful and tough. They sound like no others to me. I celebrate the publication of an excellent collection.

Elizabeth Alexander

Acknowledgements

All praise to God who gives me strength and all the words (Exodus 4:10–11).

I am eternally grateful for sisterhood in the word from Raina J. Leon and Remica L. Bingham and Aracelis Girmay.

I owe special thanks to other poet-friends who have helped me and this project and journey grow in our own ways: Mitchell L. H. Douglas, Lauren K. Alleyne, Quraysh Ali Lansana, Matthew Shenoda, and Myronn Hardy.

Much gratitude goes to present-day writers and my former teachers: especially first, Stan Whittle, without whose unconditional support I might not ever have picked up a pen again, and Thorpe Moeckel, Michael Chitwood, Randall Kenan, and Rigoberto Gonzalez; to my Cave Canem teachers, Toi Derricotte, Cornelius Eady, Patricia Smith, Cyrus Cassells, Ed Roberson, Erica Hunt, Afaa M. Weaver, Yusef Komunyakaa, Lucille Clifton, Carl Phillips, Claudia Rankine, Colleen McElroy, and Rita Dove; to my first poetry community in North Carolina, the Carolina African American Writer's Collective—especially Lenard D. Moore, L. Teresa Church, and Ebony Golden; and to every single Cave Canem fellow whom I've adopted as my extended family—I am so blessed to have been your little sister; to everyone in my various communities and houses and churches of the word and life, you sustain me; you keep me.

I must also thank and acknowledge the force of love from my dear friends Preston C. Anderson, Syhaya A. Smith, Brian K.

Lee, Abrina Brown, Jamie Efird, Jessica Forman; I remain grateful to my spiritual families and my many brothers and sisters in the Lord's name.

I have to thank those who have transitioned before or during this project, in the words of mama Sonia Sanchez: "I have called your name so there is tomorrow": Griffin E. Dameron, Annie W. Dameron ("Grandma Griffin"), Olive S. Dameron, Quincy Carr, James E. Melvin ("Papa James"), and Georgia Mae Briggs ("Grandma Georgia").

I also owe a "thank you" to Kwame Dawes for friendship and perpetual guidance.

And finally I would like to thank Elizabeth Alexander, who saw something in my work, in this collection. I am grateful.

Some of the poems presented here originally appeared in the following publications.

PMS: PoemMemoirStory—"How Quickly the Sun Comes"
42opus—"Ad in the *Chicago Defender*" and "Consider This"
    (previously titled "Only If")
The Ringing Ear: Black Poets Lean South—"Israelites"
Cave Canem Anthology XI—"Too Late to Uncapture"
Warpland—"Requiem for the Gulf Coast"
Bay Leaves—"Cuspidor"

Lament

Oh, how You end us.
The beginning of disaster
is the moist inside of a lie. How You
speak with fiery tongue, with smoke words. How You
hide spirits in the spaces of the house no one inhabits.
There are other silences You keep.

There are other silences You keep
about the way You will end us
or send spirits in the spaces of the house no one inhabits.
The beginning of disaster: Your
fiery tongue-speak. Words fly up in smoke,
curl inside-out to reveal the moist parts of a lie.

Inside the tender part—the stomach of a lie—
are other kept silences. How You twirl
Your fiery tongue. Your words are smoke.
But, how You'll end us,
summon spirits from inhabitable spaces
to whisper the beginnings of disaster.

Curled in the beginning of disaster,
deep inside the moist, tender parts are words
fired from Your tongue. All smoke.
Cull the spirits from the dark spaces of the house.
Cull them from the silences we keep.
God. The end of us.

You'll soon end us.
It will be the beginning of a disaster.
Speak now with Your tongue of fire and smoke words.
Unearth the underbelly of all lies.
Inside the silences You keep
are spirits in the spaces of the house

where no one dwells, in the crevices
where You'll surely end us—
here, in the silences of the house, the silences kept.
It will be the beginning and the end. Disaster
is the tender, moist center of every lie.
Still, Your tongue is fire. Our words, mere smoke.

I

It was The Light that ripped us apart and saved us.

All Hallows' Eve

Bodies move suspecting nothing.
A child pours herself into her Halloween
costume—a dead virgin with blood-painted
face—and goes door-to-door knocking.

I never wanted to celebrate the dead
this way. Mama, in her South Carolina
room, hears the oxygen tube slip
from your nose and sees your eyes
turn from her. I call to see how you are doing.
Mama picks up and puts down the phone.
The children on our separate streets
must skip in their costumes, collect candy
in the name of the gory dead.

You are as I last saw you: in the chair,
oxygen expanding your chest. Your imagined
whisper to my mother, her hand with olive oil
to your forehead. A disconnected phone
in my hand. I'd think it tragic to call
home at the time of your death, except it's not.
I'd think it bad luck you should die,
like my grandfather, in my mother's arms.
Except, I know we cannot prepare for it.

We cannot count down to the moment
of our departure.

The children rap at my door
in death suits, skeletal costumes.
Spirits and demons walk out
into the night with its raucous possibilities.
I am inside. You are no longer inside,
but traveling: this flying I'm scared
to do, this dying I fear.

We move on this way,
propelling ourselves into our fears.
Frozen on my bed, I say   *Children*
stop this death parade, Mama use your hands,
Daddy, answer the phone. But my gut says
you are gone. You are never
coming back. At midnight, the children stop
their rapturous inquiries. My father calls
in tears, crying this song I do not wish to know.

It Is Written

Daddy is approaching fifty. I fret
because it was his father's age
at death. All he desired of life
was to surpass his father.
Fifty-one is the only limit left to hurdle.

Six states away he watches his last living blood
turn rock and disintegrate. He calls,
hesitation constricts his words   *I don't know*
if you know, but   he is aware my knowledge
comes from what he wills over the line,
the distances between us.

He begins to cry   *Maybe you'll write*
a poem about   but I know he means, soon
there will be no one to tell the story.
He dictates   *It's funny, Mom never wanted to die*
in a nursing home.   She spent weeks
in his house and he washed her, fed her.
She always said 'you're a man
once but a child twice.'

He grabs the air. *My baby brother*
is a child twice. He cannot live
in his own house.

I don't mention karma or God's vengeance,
how Grandma couldn't spend her last days
at home because the same brother refused
to care for her. *He is going—*
I fill the blank with: *to die?*
But the space is: *to a nursing home.*
Daddy whimpers   *His skin is falling off his legs,*
he cannot care for his self.
I think about the law of God. An eye for an eye.
He starts again: *Maybe you'll write—*
And I say *Yes, yes.*

Body, an Elegy

Suddenly the body says night.
                                Cyrus Cassells

The body is not
an insomniac, some
twilight sleepless walker.
It turns to lie down
as it pleases, at times
against your will.

The body chooses
its separate departures
to backrooms of the house.
Goodnight heel, boomerang
of bone and tendons.
Goodnight feet, arch-less
pestle-crush of earth.

The doctors come
to chop you down
and cover you with strips
of white linen. See,
your legs, your trunks
of redwoods stripped
of their flesh bark

are endangered. Goodnight
kidney, fallen already
to a deep coma,
needing machines to eat
and drink. For it,
there is no waking.

Your left arm long
retired and under the
sheets. Uncle, lay
your perfect right
that never knew shunt
or needle, lay it down
so the I.V. can land. Together,
we say goodnight to the heart
that has failed you once.

But the eyes, they refuse.
Your mouth does not
wish to go so soon. So
speak your farewells, Uncle.
Speak your hundred more
farewells. Watch this holy
body of birds flap
across your window.

Oiling the Joints

Because you are unable
I will palm a dab of lotion

or Vaseline, rub rosebud salve
into the ashened, cross-hatched epidermis
let the scent linger. I will trace

my fingertip pads over your calloused knuckles
with my own, turn, smooth out your fist,

smile at the dimples. I will
continue this—my palms pressing against

pressing into, smoothing the lubricant between us.
Because you are unable, I will use

my fingertips, reach between the valley of your knuckles
and rest—my hands enmeshed between yours
oiling the joints jutting out.

Get up, I will think but not say, knowing you cannot hear.
Get up so we can bring you home.

The Last Touch

There is a dead mother
and a living daughter and the ritual
of washing hair. I was too young to think
anything heroic about her heavy head
in your hands before the funeral.
What an intimate farewell: you
waiting at the house of a friend,
the funeral home—agreeing to your request—
delivers great-grandma Georgia
so that yours could be the last touch.
How you moved your fingernails
between her wet follicles, shielded
her eyes, careful not to splash
shampoo because you remember
being chided about the burn. You denied
the embalmer's offer to dress her;
denied her their orange lipstick, but
gave her the best dress and a heel—
having been a while since she could walk
after diabetes snatched half a leg.
This intimate farewell: you rubbing
her down in baby oil, whispering
Mama, singing her those thousand hymns
ever ready in your mouth.

Cuspidor

We knew his lungs would fail
when doctors produced a picture of the defiant lump.

We denied him those delicate killers
and his elixir—slender silver barrels of beer.

It was only after our symphony of reprisal
that he left cigarettes alone. Unbelievers,

we searched the house for evidence
of his refusal, sniffed smoke

traces hovering his head like a halo.
Long after his death

we found remnants of his secreting
in Grandma's china vase—its cerulean

patterns embossed on kiln-fired ceramic. Inside:
her dried eucalyptus, his chewed tobacco twine.

Communion

WINE. n. Fermented grape-juice known to the Women's Christian
Union as "liquor," sometimes as "rum." Wine, madam, is God's next
best gift to man.

                              The Devil's Dictionary

Because we are all sinners
and, in our sinning, continue
to sin, and in our cleansing

we are sinners still—being forgiven
over and over ad infinitum

while drinking the blood
of the Son of man.

Because we can get drunk
off our Savior,

we march, stumble
the aisles to purify
wash away—

because we can begin again.

Backseat Savior

My mother believes I wish her dead. I don't
tell her how many times I have saved her
while seated on the blue-carpeted hump
of Daddy's white Lincoln, legs straddling
the tongue of the console which always
held my Hardee's cup, limp from condensation
and heat that coaxed my mother and sister
to sleep. I don't count the times
we'd driven from Charleston, late,
or that I was the only one ever wide
awake. I don't know that I considered
I could die those nights, that we could.
In the womb of the car, windows muted
by rain and four bodies breathing up
I-26, I utilized my gift of managing
insomnia and learned to watch my dad's
profile for signs: his head a weight rocking
back to the cradle of the headrest, or
a blink held some seconds too long.
Only once have I failed their faith
in my ability to get us home safely,
because I had run out of questions
and preferred the monotonous
mile-marker counting and let
the car drift down the sideline

of the two-lane highway and onto
the grated shoulder of the road and no one
flinched and I counted to five and still
his eyes were closed, his neck bent.
Maybe it's thankfulness that we grew
so close after, because in the sixth second
I found my voice and my hand on his arm,
shaking. I found that I didn't want death
for anyone. I wanted my bed, a bed for my father.
Mostly, I wanted daylight to come.

Black Saw-Wing

I do not wait for the push
never minded buzzards
who wished me over
nest's edge.
Never figured wings
could miscalculate.

Found, beak-buried.
Bellies scavenge ground.
Bones tell
the thing that never flew.

On Seeking the Other ²/₅ Up North

after Patricia Smith, based on her nineteenth-century portrait

First thing you do when you find free
is pose, take a picture in the stiff double-breasted
overcoats buttoned to the top.

First thing you do when you find free
is wash up, scrape years of top soil
baked onto skin, pray the grime in the bottom
of the basin (years' work in the dirt) can be forgiven.

You find free from southern sun,
take pictures, pose like white men, and even build
a house with mantles; dangle from the walls.

Yes, you slip your right hand
into the jacket up to the second
knuckle, just between the buttons,
snug like love into an envelope.

You pose, don't mention anything
about your roots, no, they have cut
your hair so close your scalp can breathe.

You will not smile.
Your look will be a flash into history:
your proof you made it out those fields.

Meditation

Seneca Village (Central Park, NYC)

These old bricks, lain square, are all that's left
of us. Our long ago blood lived here
once. In this space as small as a pillbox
or card case, families must have gathered around

a hearth, the fire's heat drawing them close.
Perhaps your blood came to this entryway
to request my goat's milk or an egg from a chicken
out back or conversation or love. And I wonder

if the day was as warm as it is now. Almost a century
later, I stand at the threshold, demanding history
reveal what happened to us and our kin, or
why now we must be strangers and estranged

when perhaps my blood darkened this threshold
and it was yours. These bricks must have stacked
up high enough to hold a roof. I would have stood
before you to ask for temporary shelter or work

or friendship or family. Given our conditions then,
the door was always open to each of us

and our separate skins were forgiven. We have been
segregated by more than this park erected

over our lives and I find it funny how history dissolves
the ligaments that held the bones together. How,
after time, the body can be disassembled and taken apart
bone by disconnected bone. And we forget

we cohabited once. I know the passage of time
commands I recognize my blackness and you
can now claim your whiteness. History
is the erosion of the ribbon tied around us;

I cannot hold you today for fear
of our differences, though once—
once we were corralled here. Before the park.
Before the grass and dogwoods

and tulips came. Before all we shared and were
was this barely visible foundation
of a house that is stepped over and on
and passed by without being seen.

Questions from the Jamaican Children

Buff Bay, Jamaica

What are you doing here, with them?
Najae, Teina, Crystalina ask me
with eyes that say I'm no different.
And if so, there is truth:
I came to the islands,
one of twelve, one black paraded by whites
to Jamaica, to Buff Bay with trinkets and verses.
If I was righteous, they deduced,
then so, vicariously, were they.
But when I opened my mouth,
they ran. There was something
we shared, some collective fear.
Maybe it was the composition
of my cheekbones they read instead
of my accent, my eyes in place of my mouth,
the way they look at the children—
begging to be recognized, set apart
from the rest of the other missionaries
in front of Gideon Educational Centre.
Standing as if an auction block,
I was seen, but not seen;
there and oceans away.

Ad in the Chicago Defender

after Rose Piper's "Slow Down Freight Train"

broad shouldered negro
seeks work up north.
robust hands good
for ferrying heavy loads
across long distances.
legs trained to walk
forty years in southern
wilderness. never worked
in the industry but willing
to learn. can keep long hours
slaving under intense sun.
no stranger to labor
or low wages however
there is word your low
is my promise. don't need
much room. just a corner
of a corner to rest my eyes.
will not be distracted
by women or necessity
of the loins. will travel solo.
respond soon. will board
the next north-bound train.

The Leaving

If we had time enough, my left hand
would float to the nape of your neck,
smooth the globe knot I imagine
as jade or something cool to touch.

If we could stay in this microcosm
called summer, my tongue would traverse
the terrain just behind your ear. It would
curl to the vale below the apple, flicker
the landscape, lap the salt and delight.

This rapture would be called morning.
I would hesitate to walk from our secluded
universe, sweat careening the creases

like a river where your lips taste—
and you wait with figs and persimmons.

Consider This

after Rose Piper's "Slow Down Freight Train"

If windy nights in
that blustering city

are unbearable and you find
work is not worth walking solo;

if you need the surety
of relentless kudzu

spreading miles along
country highways

and my musk scent has
lifted from my lace

you took
because you need

to remember why you're
there;

if the salt-cured ham glazed
with honey is no longer

my sweet sweat on your
tongue and your fingertips

forget journeys along my
forever hips;

if you can find someone
to stew you neck bones and

when after a search for every
remnant of flesh your lips

covet the straight lines
of my neck

then, come back.
Come back home.

II

There are blows in life so violent—I can't answer! / Blows as if from the hatred of God.

Excavation

for David

When I saw it burrowed
in the closet, I rummaged beneath
mounds—unpaired socks, bills—
in dark, damp crevices.
I did not know how to decipher
those announcements, cards, news clips.
I placed the picture of him in my lap as if
I had given birth. I felt something escape
me, your secret held for twenty-seven years.
Hello brother David, I said, half-expecting
a coo from a newborn encased in plastic
and envisioned you, torn apart,
age eleven, in a sterile hospital room
hearing Grandma yell push, Grandpa
holding your hand, praying
it would be over soon enough.
I shuffle death certificates, sympathy cards.
I bury him again.

Inheritance

after Lucille Clifton

Frequented in dreams
by fresh-dead loves, so I have seen
with these eyes the eyes of a spirit
who has crossed, seen the body reject
its coffin bed and climb right out
onto the church's plank floor
seen the dove at the bed's foot
calling out all names, or the red eyes
of the flesh, abandoned. Do not say
I should be grateful for perfect eyes
or their ability to see such distances.
Say I should be grateful for sight,
for open and shut.

My Grandfather Wouldn't Know Me If He Saw

this is what I do now: cigarette in my right hand,
tequila in my left. Double-fisting death. Slowly

the chambers of my lungs grow sinew-less,
surrender to tar and fiberglass and silence.
Does Daddy suspect I am guilty of killing myself?

Mama turns your face to avert the destruction.
Grandpa's specter arrives in the bottom of the bottle
I swore off the day I watched him walk away

from this life. Torrent of ash and smoke,
my blurred vision and smile is an illusion
I am happy left behind. Name the space once filled

a rattling gourd in my center. What I do
to get closer, to arrive here: pull from vices
an escape. What isn't final, approaches.

A bit of remorse is in order. I can't see
past this haze. Clairvoyance is a gift
I won't accept.

Underneath the Brown

We were digging for the road
to Hell. We picked up pieces
of the tree's dress, small woodchips
covering the playground.
Underneath the brown, damp
clusters, more brown: dirt
and earthworms. It wasn't enough.
We wanted depth, to see the inside
of the earth, our hands blackened
trying to continue.
There must be something else.
There must be someone else.

Once, my mother told me the Devil
was under the earth, that I was the Devil,
that all evil was held in the heart.
When we reached the red clay, we stopped.
Was this Hell? It wasn't so bad after all.
The Devil was nowhere to be found.
Maybe we were disappointed.
Maybe we gave up when all we could tell
was that below the earth's brown skin,
the black, was red. Just red.

I Heard It, Once

Union Square, NYC

In the day I ventured into the city
that claims insomnia, I heard
a sound at my back, a brick wall of sound,
like a clean whistle or a teakettle, heated.
It came and left. It was a slap to the ear.
It came again, and I turned on the park bench.
It was a man's mouth that belted out
this wail of a noise like the hum

of a machine—something non-human,
non-living. It was a vowel like *e* and *i* and *o*.
It was akin to the sound my grandmother made
when exorcising demons. I looked to be sure,
and here he was: performing an exorcism
in the middle of the park. No one found alarm.

He could have been Jesus, I thought, except
for his blond dreads, cargo pants and painted shirt.
But then, I meditated on the parable
of the well woman, some story about faith
and disbelief, this idea that Jesus—of all people—
could show up when you least expect it,
and present eternal life and water
that could flow for centuries. Why not this man

in front of the blue-suited woman waiting to be saved?
She was on her knees, a sinner. She was crying
and this man, this spiritual healer was howling.

Could he move spirits? I was not convinced
by his convulsions—having seen grown folk fall
at the feet of sweaty, suited preachers
with a sprinkle of holy water. Why was I not
convinced by his impromptu sanctuary
in the middle of the park, in front of the inch of grass
that, too, is a miracle in this cement universe
full of people not wanting, but yearning
to believe, as if a sound alone—
a vowel, a wail—were enough?

Parable of the Hungry Missionary

Buff Bay, Jamaica

1. Dinner time. I sit next to a girl
who approaches the plate as if a venereal disease.
2. She looks to the Jamaican cook who smiles, bows,
tells us it's a delicacy, this fish, its flesh roasted pink
as the girl's face flushed in disgust.
3. I accept the offering. Bow back
to thank Mr. Green.
4. How privileged we must have been
to dine at our hosts' table while they stood, watching.
5. I taste surprisingly sweet flesh set before me
folded in foil pockets, despite eyes that tell me no.
6. I look around the table, survey the twelve,
and I wonder if at the Last Supper, the Apostles
sat with hands in their laps in strong silent protest?
7. Or if, while feeding the Multitudes, the hungry
told Jesus they don't eat like this, and if he was
such a Miracle Worker, could he please remove
the eyes before setting fish before them,
expecting them to eat?

To the Man Whose Name Is "Paradise"

Dear Mr. Thenmalai,
What a beautiful name. What
a musical, rhythmic name. What's in
these names we have? This process
we use to call things? Like God bringing
animals to Adam so they can live
by their chosen names.

Like Adam, my grandmother took careful
consideration in sealing her children's fate:
My father, Thomas, agnostic or non-believing,
used the language of believers to weave
fantasy as my gospel truth.

What is the prophecy of your name,
Mr. Thenmalai? I've tried to construct
meaning from these syllables, sever
it into parts: One a term for condition
as in, "If there is rain *then*
carry an umbrella." The other half
could be Hindi for meditation or prayer. Saying
your name is prophecy like, "If the world
is ending, *then pray.*"

I've discovered your name is the appellation
of a place I imagine is Heaven, is paradise,

is "honey hills." So I must ask, Mr. Thenmalai,
is this land where you have culled
your calling where the bees have retreated?

There are no bees in this city.
I've waded in artificially-flowered parks, waiting
for one to land on my bare foot and test
my patience, my ability to restrain fear
of something so infinitely small but finitely
important to our existence. There are no bees.
Do not say it is because Fall has descended
upon us. Do not say it is because autumn
is the metaphor for dying. We know
there should be more bees.

I've come to accept my gift of prophecy, to see
things before they are done. Once, I dreamt
the world collapsed like a card house. Albert
Einstein called forth: *No more bees,*
no more pollination, no more plants, no more
man.

I meditate on the absence of bees
and do not want to believe we are ending so soon.

I want to know they have migrated
to your highlands, away from the honey-combed
skyscrapers and wax flowers. They must
be in the honey hills, bathing in the thousand
gardenias, black-eyed susans, morning glories, daisies.

The City of Discarded Umbrellas

Why do assemblies of umbrellas
always occur in London?
          Neruda, The Book of Questions

There are assemblies of the shattered
in Harlem, too. Umbrellas, broken
in the trashcans, upended

on the sidewalk, teeter
on the curb, the lip of a city under siege.
There are assemblies of abandoned umbrellas
that have given up their dance,

cannot twirl their skirts
above the heads of their travelers.
Even in the rain, in the relentless
beating of the sky, they congregate

on the corners with broken legs,
with broken backs, their feet calloused, unable to walk.

Even the Clouds Came to Gather

for Gloria Jean Brown, age fourteen

Oxygen masks delivered empty
packages to your heart's doorstep.

What good was breathing when your blood
battled against you? The day you departed,

the sky was deceptive—the sun too bright
for grieving. Funny how life masks

our entrances and exits. When it hit
like a brick to my stomach, though,

birds dropped from the sky, and even
clouds came to gather a wreath over the garden

just opening its eyes to the days ahead.
Then sudden rain. When the cool breeze

came, I wanted to give you the wind
back, to fill your lungs again with air.

Heartland of Columbia Nursing Home

After the operation, doctors said her heart was retiring,
would not send blood down the right leg.

There was no other option.

When we visited the nursing home,
I pushed the button to raise her head

toward the bent straw leaning over the cup's lip.
She asked for other favors: one more pillow

to the pile, a louder radio to hear God's word,
a yellow salty cornstarch snack in her mouth

to dissolve on her tongue, my fingernails
along her right calf.

I was confused. I moved to pat her left,
blanketed foot. I was seven and did not know the
   itch of absence.

Israelites

1.

The house my grandmother built
was sacred. *Only the Lord*,
she professed, resided within its walls.
There, she marked her doors like the Jews in Egypt,
etched *the blood of Jesus* on entryways,
red stains—sacrificial Blood —
her protection for firstborn son,
man of the house, her heir,
and controller of the legacy she'd leave.

Decades she prayed against harm's approach,
shielded against Satan's wrath with air-cross
drawn through whispered psalms.
She sung sorrows, as David did,
to her Father. Warrior, she fought
battles beyond this physical realm.

2.

Grandma, they're going to sell
the sanctuary you built, ark
for those torrential storms you
waded through. Those words will

vanish, I know. Greed's got an offering
so glorious—the lands of your Jerusalem
will be turned over soon. Let your tongues
stir up the angels you used to call upon.
Guard our souls. The place of peace
you promised is vanishing. Tomorrow,
we may be a people with no home.

Transfiguration of Jesus in Jamaica

Brother and sisters in Christ clad
in lemon-meringue shirts—Americans

eager to escape the states. Armored
with gilded, leather-bound Bibles,

we cross seas in the name of higher callings—
this twelve-passenger caravan

on Spring Break pilgrimage. Mission:
bring Gospel to Caribbean Natives.

Upon the Blue Mountain tops we will
confuse Jamaica Jah with our God

misconstrue Rastafari's i-n-i's, create our own
translation of Jah guide: *May [our] God be with you.*

We will hand out granola bars
and God bless you's two-by-two—just

like brother Noah. Our pamphlets
will profess beliefs to those that read,

and for those that can't, plastic toys
and gifts to associate redemption

with sidewalk chalk, Tonka, Barbie.
Some cannot accept this version of Jesus,

or Jah-in-flesh yet, nor the occasion of this visit—
foreign mystics making mischief

talking of change, revolution,
miracles, the promise of something more.

Condition: If the Garden of Eden Was in Africa

Having learned
they had been lied to;
having tasted bitter knowledge
and flirted with forked-tongue
soothsayer who sought to make a deal
from their flesh—after it was too late
to renege, who walked first
through that gate no longer blind—
having seen what they were leaving,
what would still be theirs,
and not dust and desert
if they could have stayed?

To the Black Girl in Charleston, SC, Waving the Confederate Flag

Steal away, steal away, steal away, steal away . . .

In Dixie, the cobblestones will trip you
if you travel too fast as you are, skipping down
a narrow street, crowded with carriages and horses.
Barely room for cars, I ride my bike from here

to there, and stop to see you: sepia in a sea of beige,
one lone wild grain in a glass jar of white. Midday,
a school day, you wear a magenta backpack.
Your uniform is pleated and pressed. Because you,
Sister, are here on this street I pass through, I am convinced

you are not a local—one who respects boundaries
like a dog tethered to an invisible chain. Already,

my observation is biased and imbalanced, having immediately
pitted black against white, having
compared humans to animals. But we are, at times,
animal-like—conditioned to fear our masters

if we venture beyond our sequestered kingdoms.
This city would have us believe we don't belong.
Here you are: holding a Confederate flag souvenir,

waving the criss-cross blue bars of stars over red.
It is a kite trailing as you negotiate Broad
and Market Streets. Watching you, I know you must

be foreign to this world of *do nots* and *yes sirs*.
You head south of East Bay by the waterfront
in the belly of this Holy City, near the harbor
having purchased only this to mark your travels.

Missionaries Lead the Children in First Steps

Buff Bay, Jamaica

When my team first assumed
the children non-believers, Jamaican infidels,
more black, faithless followers
of some false decree, they set out
to teach otherwise.

They prepared pastorals, nursery rhymes,
bracelets to visualize the concept.

There was no question of holiness
in this activity, in a small brand around
the wrist—personal stairway to heaven.

In the chaos of activity time, they climbed
the ladder of hemp and seven beads
so the children could know God like they believed:

Black, they explained first, is Sin.
White, is angelic. The color of God.

Lynching Mobs

after Gertrude Abercrombie's "Charlie Parker's Favorite Painting"

They come to the hanging tree
in Sunday best: pressed white shirts, satin gloves.
Come to watch the spectacle, pay a dollar
to view genitalia, climb the ladder
to light the match. The noose
hangs from strongest branch. Rituals by full moon.

They gather under the moon's
glare. Here, they've picked the perfect hanging tree.
One man fondles the rungs of the noose.
He holds the circle with gloves
about the head. He stays close, leans against the ladder.
The view from there is well worth his dollar.

To watch fire strip skin from bones, a dollar.
Witness the skeleton set ablaze, crumble beneath the moon.
Bring the charred remains down by ladder,
Do not venture far from the tree.
Redress the naked corpse, offer clean gloves,
a hat, suspenders, necklace: a noose.

No, they never remove the noose
from the neck. A man offers cash
for his picture taken with the woman in satin gloves.

They pose (how romantic: a backdrop, the moon)
with the hanged man leaning against the tree
propped up as if sitting on the ladder.

Men gather around the dead and the ladder,
take turns holding up the noose.
Their arms simulate a branch of the tree.
Take a picture, flash a dollar.
Smile wider than the open moon
suspended over the lone nebula. And the gloves!

The woman's pink satin gloves
setting gingerly about the ladder—
pink reflecting the light of the full moon.
And too, the nameless black body is strangled by the noose
before the lone abandoned dollar.
Still here, this tree, this dying hanging tree.

Tree's Memory

after Gertrude Abercrombie's "Charlie Parker's Favorite Painting"

1. nebula

embossed in the eternal
background: heated air
congeals, levitates.
where does
the spirit go when
it leaves the body?

2. noose

thirteen rungs, jute-twisted
collected around its source
ensures clean snap when
snatched, my arm pulled
to the earth & back.
the weight of them;
rope caught in the space
between vertebrae,
folds the neck in half.
how the head bows
to the right.

3. ladder

people want to reach
his level—they climb
the rungs to catch the eyes
before pupils glaze over with death

4. touch

a woman wants bare
hands to feel the penis
that dangles from the boughs
before carved from the carcass.
she removes her satin gloves,
caresses the penis
grating against the shaft
with longing—
the men let her.
they laugh. they laugh
knowing the memory
invoked by touch

5. full moon

God's lone open eye

Prelude to Death

after Moyo Okediji's "The Dutchman"

Elders preached this—
dreamt of smoke and woke up

sweating. Pulled fresh from the Atlantic.
Bodies glide towards us

creep closer up-shore like summer tide.
They speak with fire in their mouths,

with walking stick that bangs.
They come in hut-shaped helmets

in long clothes that shield all.
Our breasts are bare and lactating.

One of them looks as if to drink.
White hands are locked

cuffs around our wrists.
We know them possessed,

read the smoke rising from
their lips. Summoning

spirits. Whose ghosts are haunting us?

Requiem for the Gulf Coast

The water has receded.
Crows come in their funeral dress

to wade in mud and filth, feast on
bodies of those who could not flee.

It was a dream ago. Still,
crows find food, forage
the land we cannot touch.

We cannot return to reclaim
our names rinsed away by rain.

Our home is a wasteland.
We crawl the streets of foreign towns
looking to settle. We ward off

ones who come in guile to snatch
what remains. We dream a city
whose light will withstand waves.

Buff Bay, Jamaica

It is not Kingston, riled with gunfire symphonies
or Red Stripes that surround the cityscapes
like yellow caution tape.

It is not the beaches' advertisements for Spring Break
escapades. Not even the lure of ganja in
marketplaces. The preaching of no worries: smoking

grass religion. But it is the turquoise smell
of ocean, and breadfruit, the eternal reggae
off-beat thumping in the distance;

the intriguing mystery of nighttime travels
without streetlamps, the uninhibited lands
with roadways like labyrinths; a never-ending path

to the other side nestled between Ocho Rios and
Montego Bay. It is my new haven with mountain-top
coffee growers, goats' bleats, coconut

trees sprouting like weeds. Yes. It is the children's
versions of our American hand games, nursery rhymes,
and rap songs, to Jesus—molding new what was left

of those who came before us, and after.

Too Late to Uncapture

It was not that you posed or paused
for the camera flash reflected in your eyes.

You did not flutter or join
your brethren's dolorous chatter.

It was not that I was suspicious of walking
between the worlds while documenting

your transition—the way we snatch souls
of our living to anchor memory

when they cross over. It is summer,
the wrong season for dying. But here you are.

The breeze comes, and the ants in their steps
to carry you away. I am sorry.

I want to rescind my voyeuristic alchemy
of light and shutter and click.

Divining

This morning I circle a magnolia, wait
long enough for her—sage
with dried tobacco-colored skin.

I rest a tongue-leaf in my hand. Conjure
Grandma kneeling at the base of a magnolia
in South Carolina, in her suburban backyard.

Here, at the root of this lone magnolia I think:
more blossoms. Spring in North Carolina
is nothing like home. Home praises

these evergreen monuments, not dogwoods
who shower their stench—petals falling like snow—
getting all hallelujahs. I run my fingers along the tongue-leaf's

crease. Grandma's mouth. How I miss it,
peppered with long-ago stories. Though
I think it when I come, I am not alone.

A robin rests beside me. Grandpa:
The red-breast chest shield flashes in glory.

III

We recognize the sources of our hunger.

Mala Is for Meditation

Focus is required.
The mind and heart are known to wander.
Anchor your meditations
with 108 beads in the right hand.

Do not let the mind and heart wander.
Origami-fold legs, one hand over heart
the other must hold 108 beads.
Your index finger cannot touch the mala.

The first bead is sumeru. Begin:
What can I do on a daily basis to bring peace?
Move beads in rhythm with this mantra.
How can I bring peace where there is violence?

Repeat: *What can I do on a daily basis to bring peace?*
Continue loop until the summit is reached.
Ask again: *How can I bring peace where there is violence?*
At the 109th bead, continue your pace,

Pause at sumeru. Some prayers need repeating.
Roll the beads between middle finger and thumb.
Reflect on your journey. Reverse. Begin your steps again:
What can I do on a daily basis to bring peace? What can I do . . .

Rolling the beads between middle finger and thumb
anchors your hundred meditations.
If you wish to bring peace on a daily basis
know that focus is required.

Landslide in La Jolla

October 4, 2007

Dear Soledad Mountain,
Forgive my tardiness: I should
have no reason for this late letter except
disbelief in the failure of our footings—

that our rock could crumble and slide,
that we could be rinsed away in the rising

waters. Is it true, though, what the headlines
proclaim? Our earth yawned open to swallow
whole the houses, the trees, the telephone lines?

I have come to understand how sick things operate,
their changes so subtle they go unnoticed until
it is too late and the remnants are ghosts,

and in their place, regrets. What they say
happened is not unusual—the ailing body

in its graduated diminuendo cannot stop
its cheek's concave or their bones' convex.

Still, as I have seen, the sick
skeletons acquiesce to the weight
of the outside pressure pressing

inward and can no longer hold
the skin, its outer shell. It can only collapse.

Bless

for Olive Salomé

consider God's apology:
an olive branch in a dove's mouth

or the oil in the lamp
offering light   days after promise
in His temple

I know what it is like to be the blackest child
and outcast   with sepia firm flesh
I know the hard pitted inside

you were named after a tree with impossible fertility
and it was prophecy   your barren center

Aunt Olive   you kept me
claimed me knowing you would never
have your own seeds to plant and flourish

there is no peace without the offering of your name

Olive, I say   tongue peeking
through my teeth   the word round
like the world and tangible

to speak your name is to anoint   bless
when I utter your name   prayer

Ode to the Camel-Hair Brush

Hard-handled tamer
of wild things,
Mama once kept
you
with her. Always,
in the holster
of her purse,
ready
to charge the fields,
you with your thousand
army rakes, combing
through the bush,
thorough
you crawl
onward,
upward,
outward, your flat face
against my ears
whispering how you
will break me, how
I will lay down
and be still, never rise
up against you.

Closer to Knowing

after Phillip Levine

I kneel in my porcelain tub
thigh-deep in water to wash three weeks'
worth of clothes. I can't say
I know now what work is but I might
be closer to knowing sacrifices my elders
made—domestics on the Battery—
hand-cleansing filthy clothes—
hours of rubbing knuckles together—
to get the friction needed
in large metal contraptions
of detergents and softeners to rinse
clean our daily sweat and dirt. Growing up
will do this, I suppose. I find
myself on a Saturday night forced
to forfeit amenities. Working up
a sweat—my hands softened and rubbed raw
at once—I wring the privilege
from too many pairs of jeans. I am thankful
for this meditation in the bathtub, this homage.
Maybe work is laboring for a dime, for three children

and an absent husband. Work is a stranger's
intimates between your fingers
plunged down below the suds
and lifted to the light.

Portrait of a Seafarer

This is what has become of him:

curled bones in the ocean's mouth,
his body tossed like blasphemy.

He is a man on his knees
in the ship's belly

come to this rapture of rainfall
and flaying winds a broken thing.

Around him, all endings:
the plank floor creaks its surrender.

Sails whistle as they flap,
collapse onto themselves. He imagines

the shore of his life swallowed
by rising waters. Only his mother's

Bible words come to him in this hour
as he refuses comfort.

This is not how he contemplated coming to God.

His eyes ache for the amber moon
he knows watches on stiller nights.

Polaris between his eyes, he says
Look where you've brought me

and ponders the path back to the beginning
of his journey. *One more night*

he chants *One more night.*
Faith a provision abandoned.

The Body as a House

after Forest Hamer

Say the body is not full of the spirit
Say the spirit does not exist.
    Repent.
Say there is no such thing as the rapture
       and live your days on middle ground.

Say there is no such rapture.
Say the mouth is a portal between heaven and earth,
       that the eyes bring in or shut out the light,
       that the ears harbor a song with which to dance.

Say I live in the body in order to dance.

Say your body is only flesh
       and not a house of habitable organs.
       Repent. You should not say it.

Say the body is imperfect and love it still.
      The body is, in fact, imperfect, but
say you love it, as I do.

The Space Between

When I decided to leave the house
I tell my family I'm never coming back.
I tell my father he is free,
he can live his life. *Thank you*
I say *for staying.* I don't consult my mother
on this, because my fleeing is her fault;
she ran me out with her callousness, her inability
to love so close without killing. It has taken me
this long to understand her love
only works from a distance, that the closer we are
the harder it is to breathe. Maybe I knew
this when I told my father to step away
so my parents could love each other better. Distance
has made me understand I love
like my mother, that I keep things
too close until they are dead, gone.
My mother told me once
I'll never know how to love a man.
I spent my days trying to prove her wrong
and found myself calling from six states away
to tell her I slept with a man who broke my heart.
You should have kept him apart until you knew
she says. *Made him wait. I should have made your father*
wait. I can't say I know if he ever loved me.

The Red Thread

He rests his lips on my forehead, fondles
a lock of hair. My cheek on his chest
we swim in currents of dreadlocks

converging in the delta of his arm stretched
flat across his pillows. My right hand weaves
our strands together like birds building

nests in azaleas. He says he can see
I carry a world on my head, that my hair
holds the weight of many lovers. Our hair

is a bird's nest, I think, an ephemeral
construction, the disparate gathered to build
a bed. I want to know if birds are monogamous,

if there is such a thing as lovebirds, except
this act, this bed, might know nothing
of love or eternity. He picks up the South African

wooden bead lost in my black jute vines,
the twisted ropes, twirls it in a question
he won't ask. He says he's always hated red.

I don't tell him I've pulled new burgundy
threads from his locks already, how we pick up
and carry all our lives everywhere we go. I want

to know why it will end like this—his lock offering
more than he'll offer in words. I don't tell him
I know there is someone else, that he holds

the energy of all the women he's loved in this bed,
in his hair. I believe I should abandon him,
and too, I have collected the jerseyed sheets,

his camel-brown wool, his raven skin—
all the places I have last lain my head.

How Quickly the Sun Comes

I know my phone vibrates
before it rings. I stop it before it wakes you.
The red light is still on. I start to curl out of bed
to the corner where I abandoned my clothes.

Everything on my body is awake
in the chill of the house. I lift my arms,
clothes cascade my body. I want to crawl back
into your cradle. I stop to think

how little we talked; how quickly it came to this.
The sun is rising. You are not. Slowly, I pull
my jeans over my hips. You are on your back,
slight snore. I watch you like this

a moment longer. I reach for my shoes
and want you to turn over and reach for me.
I want for your arm to arch, your hand falling
to your side in search of my waist. I wonder

about the light still on, un-needed with this dawn.
At the threshold of your house,
the damp-dew smell reminds me of hours before.
I get in the car and know I will never greet

your sleeping self in the morning again.
I am home now. I have lost your number.
I finger the empty space where my rings were.
I wonder how long you will keep them.

Wednesday Night Fish Fry

Harlem, NYC

a fried-flounder offering: bow your heads: open
note: amen: this night: full-moon basement jam:
low lights: bass clarinet's high-range ululations: mothers
and fathers two-step: twirl: two-step with hands raised:
guttural holler: low: *yeah* and *yeah* and *blow baby*: *blow*:

in the twilight-hour dervish: chord inferno:
the temperature rises: pyre despite wintry mix: this
hollow house-music: chamber, conjure up these tired
    bones: testament

of sorrow: come clean: shake loose
the beast who comes: ward it off
horn: rebuke it organ: speak tongues, drums

Thursday Morning

Light flickers and refracts off the copper-coiled ring
on your marriage finger. I consider these things—

where we place objects on our bodies to tell stories.
Seated alone in the audience, I am undone

each time your fingers compress
the contour of your saxophone into a moan.

I want you to tell me stories about where you travel
in that moment when your eyes are closed, about

the organization of your house or if there are dishes
in your kitchen sink or women's clothing you'll explain

away when we cross the threshold together. Later,
running my fingernails across the ring's ridges, I recall

similar failed beginnings with other lovers
who adorn this space I want to occupy with a platinum

band, cover up what should be empty. I know this image—
my hands inside yours—is the short-lived ecstasy

of new beginnings, this pattern of false starts
like the other rings: royal-blue glass-bead set

into the flattened underbelly of sterling silver. Or
the cool turquoise square in pewter.

Joe Turner's Come

He said *It's all a dream baby, don't wait to sleep;*
And 'cause it's all a dream, go on, don't sleep.
You can have all you want, just reach and take a drink.

He said *Let go of inhibitions, break those chains;*
Told me *loose those inhibitions, set loose those chains.*
Between sleeping and waking, this life is all the same.

Been round the world, love, tasted each of the seven seas;
Traveled the globe, girl, just to taste the seven seas.
Back in town for a quick gig, now Sunday I'm gon' leave.

He told me his story on the ivories, massaged it on the keys;
Told me his story in black and white, fingers kissed eighty-eight
    keys.
Told it so well, I wanted that keyboard to be me. I said:

Tell me it all. I want to taste Italy on your lips;
Can I? Taste France, Brazil, Berlin, still on your lips?
Your blues, got me wantin' to live.

No Longer Ashamed

In the daylight, under the open glare
of the unshaded bulb in your apartment,

I straddle your lap. It is hot for February.
Down to tank top and bare feet you brush

your hand against my forearms, shoulders,
chest. Despite desire, I am a stone statue

in the garden. The only times we've come
to this place is under the cloak of night—

oh inscrutable night I bloom under
without pause, without question, confident

in my invisibility. You reach with cupped hand
to a breast as if to hold water. You ask

if you could see me. I am a small sip falling
between your fingers.

Flame

When you meet a man who is satisfied
with one match to start a fire

that should last one thousand days,
you want to be the wall wind

cannot pass through, to be as wide
as a brick house around his singular hearth.

When you meet this man, you want
to be the dry kindling and you wait

for the touch, the blue of his fire.
This man's love is a final flame

held over you, and you say that you will
burn. You will. Here is your body that burns

for him. Here is the ash: your used-up self,
what's left to be swept away.

This Sacrifice, This Love

I consider the Savior's
hands perfectly pierced
while seated on the downtown
redline train, next to this man
I charge with my salvation.
A selfish request I have,
wishing him to come
and lift me up, give me new
skin, promise everlasting
happiness. *Show me
your hands* I ask,
wishing to unsheathe evidence
he is flesh and ligaments,
sapphire veins and bone.
This request, biblical,
I think, turning each over
my lap, recalling Mary's
quiet fascination before Jesus'
tomb, and how she witnessed
His wounds offered up
as resurrection's proof. Running
my fingers along his spider-webbed
lines, I imagine the twelve
apostles and even poor Thomas,
like myself, unable to believe

Jesus' love reborn, requesting
more miracles and signs. I need
the opened void of puncture
wounds, someone like Him
to emerge from the damp
dark earth on third days,
to roll back the boulder and tell me
with his open hands *This is sacrifice,*
this is love and command me
to believe him.